Nathan Hale

Courageous Spy

Leaders of the American Revolution

Leaders of the American Revolution

Nathan Hale

Courageous Spy

Rachel A. Koestler-Grack

CHELSEA HOUSE
PUBLISHERS
A Haights Cross Communications ✦ Company ®
Philadelphia

CHELSEA HOUSE PUBLISHERS
VP, NEW PRODUCT DEVELOPMENT Sally Cheney
DIRECTOR OF PRODUCTION Kim Shinners
CREATIVE MANAGER Takeshi Takahashi
MANUFACTURING MANAGER Diann Grasse

Staff for Nathan Hale
EXECUTIVE EDITOR Lee Marcott
EDITORIAL ASSISTANT Carla Greenberg
PRODUCTION EDITOR Bonnie Cohen
PHOTO EDITOR Sarah Bloom
COVER AND INTERIOR DESIGNER Keith Trego
LAYOUT 21st Century Publishing and Communications, Inc.

A Haights Cross Communications ✦ Company ®

www.chelseahouse.com

First Printing

9 8 7 6 5 4 3 2 1

Library of Congress Cataloging-in-Publication Data

Koestler-Grack, Rachel A., 1973–
    Nathan Hale: courageous spy/Rachel A. Koestler-Grack.
      p. cm.—(Leaders of the American Revolution)
    Includes bibliographical references and index.
    ISBN 0-7910-8623-2 (hard cover)
  1. Hale, Nathan, 1755–1776—Juvenile literature. 2. United States—History—
Revolution, 1775–1783—Secret service—Juvenile literature. 3. Spies—United
States—Biography—Juvenile literature. 4. Soldiers—United States—Biography—
Juvenile literature. I. Title. II. Series.
    E280.H2K64 2006
    973.3'85'092—dc22

                                              2005004786

Contents

Surrender
or Die!

In the early morning hours of September 21, 1776, Nathan Hale walked into a quiet tavern at The Cedars, near New York. The tavern belonged to the widow Rachel Chichester, known to most as "Mother Chick." She was a firm and committed Loyalist. The Loyalists supported the British Army during the Revolutionary War, believing that, as loyal British citizens, they had a duty to support the British king and the British Parliament. They hated the Patriots who fought for independence and opposed their efforts to create a new nation, one that was separate from Britain.

Nathan was a Patriot captain in the Continental Army. But he when he walked into the tavern at The Cedars on that September morning, he wasn't dressed in his uniform. He was disguised as a traveling schoolteacher. For more than a week, Hale had been wandering through the British Army camps, mingling with soldiers and officers, keeping a keen eye out at all times. Hale was an American spy.

If the British discovered him, Hale would be put to death by hanging. This fate was the punishment for being a spy. Hale understood this risk when he agreed to take on the treacherous mission. For his friend and commander-in-chief, General George Washington, and for his country, he was willing to take that chance.

Walking into this enemy tavern was dangerous. But Hale did not know anyone in the area. Certainly, no one would recognize him as an American soldier. He pulled up a chair at one of the tables and ordered breakfast.

Before long, he was chatting with the other customers. Hale's easy-going personality made it easy for

Nathan Hale disguised himself as a traveling schoolteacher and wandered through the British camps, spying on the soldiers and reporting on troop movements.

him to make friends wherever he went. He was having such a good time, he almost forgot why he was there.

Hale's mission was over. He had traveled safely through hostile British-held territory, and now he was waiting for a boat to take him across the East River, where he would join his fellow Patriots. When he

Hale undertook the dangerous mission at the request of his friend, George Washington, who was serving as commander-in-chief of the Continental Army.

arrived at the dock earlier that morning, the boat was not there. Hale was famished after his long journey and decided to have something to eat while he waited for the boat.

MISTAKEN IDENTITY

Mother Chick cleared Hale's dishes away. As she turned from his table, she noticed a strange boat nearing the shore. "Who might that be?" she asked.

"Patriots!" the customers gasped. "We must hide." The men left their meals at the table and scurried toward the door.

"Nathan, come with us," one man exclaimed.[1]

"Don't worry about me, friends," Hale replied. "The patriots will not harm a quiet schoolteacher."[2]

As soon as the tavern emptied, Hale slipped out the door. He ran down to the dock, certain that the boat was for him. He was so anxious to return to General Washington with his report that he did not notice the larger ship in the distance—one with British flags. Suddenly, a dozen men jumped out of the boat. Their guns were pointed straight at Hale.

"Surrender or die!" they shouted.[3]

Test Your Knowledge

I Hale was captured in which one of the colonies?

  a. Virginia.

  b. Massachusetts.

  c. New York.

  d. New Jersey.

2 Who was considered a Loyalist?

  a. Someone who supported the British king and Parliament.

  b. Someone who supported the cause of independence.

  c. A soldier loyal to General Washington.

  d. Those in the unit of the Continental Army responsible for intelligence.

3 In order to spy on the British, how did Hale disguise himself?

  a. As a British soldier.

  b. As a traveling schoolteacher.

  c. As a journalist.

  d. As a peddler.

4 What was the punishment for spying?

  a. Imprisonment.

  b. Exile from the American colonies.

  c. Death by hanging.

  d. Death by firing squad.

5 Why did Hale hurry to the dock?

a. He believed that a boat was waiting to transport him to safety.

b. He hoped to learn more about the British naval plans.

c. He was expecting to meet General George Washington.

d. He wanted to escape from the Loyalists in the tavern.

ANSWERS: 1. c; 2. a; 3. b; 4. c; 5. a

A Special Lad

Deacon Richard Hale took out his handkerchief and wiped the sweat from his forehead. The spring sun burned hot in the clear blue sky over Coventry, Connecticut. Hale and his employees had been working the field since the first pale, pink streak of light broke across the gray sky. From his prosperous farm, Deacon Hale had a wonderful view of the budding New England countryside. For miles around, farmers were busy in their fields, barely taking a moment to enjoy the beautiful June morning.

Hale's face held an expression of anxiety. He worked his hoe down the row of corn, pausing every several yards to look towards his home. Already that morning, he had made five trips to the house to check on his wife.

Deacon Hale looked up and saw a woman running down the long slope to the field. As she drew closer, he took a deep breath and held it. The woman stopped and bent over with her hands on her knees, trying to catch her breath. "Congratulations, Deacon Hale," she gasped. "You have a sixth son. The boy is so strong Elizabeth is already calling him her finest child."[4]

With a sigh of relief, Deacon Hale clasped his hands together and raised them toward the sky. He closed his eyes and said a prayer of thanks. In those days, many mothers and infants died during the rigors of childbirth. Hale was thankful that both mother and child were in good health. Dropping his hoe, he walked with long, quick strides to the house. The young maid had to run alongside him to keep up with his brisk pace.

"You will name the baby Richard, won't you Deacon?" she breathlessly asked. "Surely after five sons, it is time to name a boy after you."[5]

"We will call him Nathan," Richard answered. He glanced over at the maid, who looked confused. "I had a kinsman named Nathan," he continued. "He was a righteous and deeply patriotic man. I will be very pleased if this child has only half of his duty and loyalty."[6] Little did Richard know that the baby boy born to him on June 6, 1755, would become one of the most courageous men in American history, a man whose name would come to symbolize duty and patriotism.

CHILDHOOD ON THE FARM

Nathan Hale's mother was Elizabeth Strong. She was thoughtful, gentle, and a lover of books. Although she had a beautiful face, she was thin and frail. She married Richard Hale when she was 18 years old.

Despite her small frame, she worked just as hard as any other housewife of the eighteenth century. She never became overwhelmed by the long days or endless chores.

Nathan was born into a strict, religious, Puritan family. His father led the children in long prayers at breakfast, lunch, and supper. Every evening, the family gathered in front of the fire to read and study the Bible. The night ended with more prayers. Nathan and his brothers scurried off to bed at 9:00 P.M. They rarely spent time whispering in the candlelight before falling asleep. They knew that their father would wake them too early.

At 4:00 A.M., Richard Hale called his sons out of bed before the sun even peaked over the eastern horizon. He expected the boys to put in a full day of work, just like the rest of the family.

Life on a farm meant long days of hard work. Like most colonial children, Nathan was expected to take care of daily chores. He helped hook up the horses to the plow. While his father led the team down the field, Nathan walked beside him. Nathan helped plant wheat and corn, weed the fields, and harvest the crops. He probably milked the cows, gathered eggs, and fed and watered the animals.

Deacon Hale was always pushing his boys and field hands to work harder. At the end of one day, he noticed that the workers were getting sluggish. They slowly threw pitchforks of hay onto a wagon. Deacon Hale jumped on top of the cart and yelled, "More hay, more hay!" He pitched so fast and with so much energy that the workers could barely keep up with his frantic pace. The pile of hay grew higher and higher. Suddenly, the pyramid toppled over. Richard tumbled to the ground, covered in hay. The workers looked at each other and began to laugh. But Deacon Hale crawled out of the mess, brushed himself off, and jumped back onto the mound. "More hay, more hay!" he shouted again.[7]

Deacon Hale opposed all kinds of board games. He thought that they were a foolish waste of time. He did not allow the boys to play with the morris board, a game similar to tic-tac-toe. To make sure that the boys behaved properly, he sat over them with a candle in his hand. Eventually, he would drift off to sleep, and the boys would quietly pull out the morris board. One brother would keep a careful watch and warn the others if their father awakened.

At the time of his birth, his mother had predicted that Nathan would be her healthiest son. But her prediction was soon proved false. When he was a toddler, Nathan suffered from terrible coughs. He eventually recovered, but he was a pale and thin child. He did not grow as tall and strong as other boys his age.

Nathan refused to let his fragile health get the best of him. Before long, he proved to be a leader in all games of skill and strength. He was an excellent runner and a champion when wrestling with his friends. Nathan loved being outdoors. His friends acknowledged him as the best hunter and fisherman. He often made their fishing rods and other hunting tools.

A LOVE OF LEARNING

Nathan excelled in other areas, as well. From an early age, he showed signs of amazing intelligence. His mother noticed that there was something special about her son, and she gave him extra attention, trying to encourage his love of learning. Deacon Hale had planned to send only his two oldest sons to college. Most colonial families could not afford to send all of their sons to college (daughters did not attend college), especially if they had a large family like the Hales. College was only thought necessary for those young men planning to enter certain professions—to become lawyers, or doctors, or clergymen.

But Nathan's mother secretly decided that Nathan would attend college. She sent him to study with Dr. Joseph Huntington, the pastor of the family's

When he was fourteen years old, Hale left home to attend Yale College.

church—the church where his father served as deacon (someone who, although not a pastor or minister, performs important duties in the church). Dr. Huntington grew quite fond of Nathan, and agreed that he was a promising young student. Nathan studied diligently and showed enthusiasm for reading and learning.

When Nathan was 12 years old, tragedy struck the Hale family. A new baby was born to Richard and Elizabeth Hale, but the newborn died. Shortly after the baby was buried, Elizabeth also became ill. Nathan's mother had lived a hard life. During 19 years of marriage, she had given birth to 12 children—nine boys and three girls. The baby who had died was the second child she had lost as an infant, and Elizabeth Hale did not long survive the loss. After a brief illness, she died.

A NEW MOTHER

Two years after Elizabeth's death, Deacon Hale remarried. His new wife was Abigail Adams. Abigail had seven children of her own, three of whom came to live with the Hales. Although many of the children were grown, the number of family members living at the Hale homestead grew to 19.

Abigail brought a more relaxed way of life to the Hale family. She wasn't nearly as strict as Deacon Hale and was more forceful in her opinions than Elizabeth had been. Nathan liked this new, lighthearted attitude. Nathan was especially fond of his new stepsister, Alice Adams. About the same age as Nathan, Alice was beautiful and petite. Her big, hazel eyes sparkled when she laughed, and her long, black ringlets bounced with every light step. In addition to her uncommon beauty, she was smart and witty in conversation. When Nathan left home to continue his education in 1769, Alice promised to write to him.

YALE COLLEGE

At the age of 14, Nathan was ready for college. In those days, it was not unusual to start college at such a young age. He left quiet Coventry for Yale College (now Yale University) in the busy, seaport town of New Haven, Connecticut. His 16-year-old brother, Enoch, also enrolled at Yale in 1769. Although Nathan wanted to study law, Deacon Hale sent both of his sons to college to become ministers.

At college, Nathan took a greater interest in sports. He was a star wrestler and broke the high jump record. He and Enoch also joined a literary group called the Linonian Society. The study group discussed topics such as astronomy, literature, and important issues of the day. Students of the society could voice their own opinions and argue their beliefs with other members. At school, Nathan was popular and made many friends. One of his closest friends was Benjamin Tallmadge. Years later, Benjamin would become a Patriot, just like Nathan.

It was at this time that Nathan probably became interested in the growing tension in the American colonies. When Nathan was growing up, Connecticut was one of 13 American colonies along the eastern coast of North America. These colonies—which stretched from Massachusetts to Georgia—were considered part of Great Britain and ruled by the English king.

But Great Britain was far away, across the Atlantic Ocean. Colonists became accustomed to governing themselves. In fact, more than 100 years before Nathan was born, the founders of Connecticut wrote the first constitution. They called it the Fundament Orders of Connecticut. This document formed the first real government in America.

Nathan believed that the colonists should have the freedom to run their own governments. He thought that Great Britain mistreated the colonists. The British government had placed taxes on supplies the colonists had to buy from Great Britain, such as paper, paint, tea, and other goods. The money collected went to pay for British soldiers and officials stationed in the colonies. These taxes were part of the Townshend Acts of 1767. Many colonists thought that these taxes were unfair.

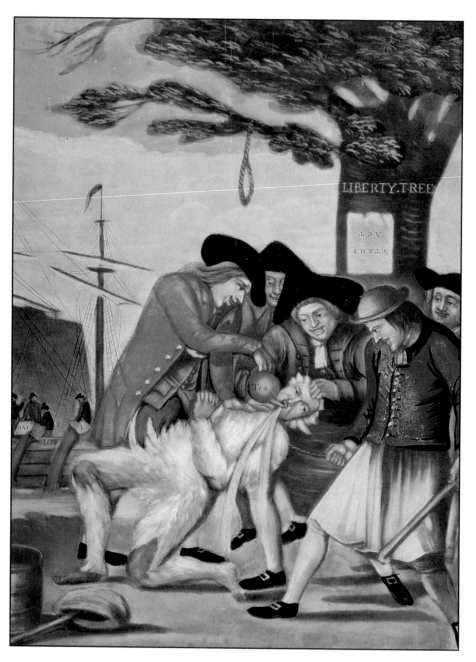

While Hale was in college, he learned of the protests against tax collectors in the colony of Massachusetts. This colored engraving from 1774 shows the taxman being tarred and feathered by a group of Bostonians.

While Nathan was at Yale, some colonists held protests against British rule. In Boston, in the colony of Massachusetts, colonists refused to pay the taxes and even attacked tax collectors. Newspapers throughout the colonies printed articles condemning Great Britain for its laws. Many merchants stopped buying goods that were imported from Britain. They chose to use products made in the colonies instead.

In 1768, Britain stationed military troops in Boston to enforce the Townshend Acts. The presence of soldiers in Boston made many colonists nervous. Many believed that this was simply a first step, leading to a full-scale military occupation of all the colonies. They worried that the arrival of British soldiers was an alarming sign of troubled times.

Despite unrest in the colonies, Nathan continued to study hard. He lived up to his motto, "A man should never lose a minute."[8] He had a special gift as an eloquent speaker. He was a wonderful master of words, and his arguments were always logical and full of common sense and elegant phrases. At times, he thought that he would be a better lawyer than a minister.

During school vacations, Nathan visited his home in Coventry. He fell deeper in love with Alice, and he finally expressed his feelings to her. (Some historians do not believe that Nathan was in love with Alice. Others think that it was Nathan's brother, Enoch, who admired her.)

When Nathan revealed his feelings, Alice told him that she was in love with him, too. They knew that they needed Deacon Hale's approval to marry, but they were sure that he would be happy for them. After all, they were not blood relatives.

To their shock and dismay, Deacon Hale firmly told them that there would be no marriage within the family. Abigail tried to get him to change his mind, but he would not be persuaded. Nathan returned to Yale broken-hearted.

In the spring of 1773, Nathan graduated from Yale. He was 18 years old and one of the 13 highest-ranked students in his class. During the graduation ceremony, Nathan Hale gave an unusual speech for a young man of that time. He spoke on the education of women. In those days, women did not receive the same educational opportunities as men. Many women could not read or write their own name.

Nathan Hale strongly felt that it was wrong to deny women a good education. He praised women and their intellect, and even though it was not a popular opinion, his speech met with tremendous applause.

EAST HADDAM SCHOOLMASTER

After graduation, Hale was anxious to find a job and support himself. He accepted an offer to teach at a school in East Haddam, a small town in Connecticut. The 18-year-old Yale graduate became a schoolmaster at East Haddam. This job must have been incredibly difficult for Hale. He taught a class of 33 students—ages six to eighteen—all in a one-room schoolhouse. During a typical school day, he instructed pupils from 7:00 A.M. until 9:00 P.M., with only one free hour at lunchtime.

Despite the long hours, Hale's students adored him. "He was a happy and faithful teacher, everybody loved him," one student remembered. "He was sprightly, kind, intelligent and so handsome."[9]

Hale enjoyed the lovely scenery of the quiet country town. But he soon missed the hustle and bustle of the city. In a letter to a friend, he complained about his "remote life in the wilderness."[10] Nathan was constantly on the lookout for something much bigger.

Meanwhile, in Boston, new trouble was boiling between the colonists and Great Britain. In colonial

America, tea was a staple beverage, much like coffee is today. Colonists loved their tea. The British East India Company controlled all trading between India and the American colonies. The British Parliament put a tax on tea brought into the colonies. Americans

The Boston Massacre

The night of March 5, 1770, was a snowy one in Boston. A couple of boys threw snowballs at each other as they ran down the darkened streets. They noticed a British soldier standing at his guard post. The boys decided to have some mischievous fun. They reached down and picked up a handful of the wet snow and shaped it into a tight ball. Then, they hurled their snowballs at the British soldiers. It was so much fun, they had to do it again.

Before long, a crowd had gathered around the boys. A snowball fight seemed like a harmless way to take their frustrations out on the soldiers. The crowd joined in the battle, too. Soon, the streets were thick with men, women, and children, all throwing snow and ice at the small cluster of British soldiers.

The British guards felt outnumbered. The crowd started shouting insults and chanting. The soldiers feared that they might be trampled by the mob. Just then,

thought it was wrong for Parliament to tax the colonies, because they did not have representatives in Parliament who could vote on their behalf. Colonists said they could not have "taxation without representation."

someone rang the church bell, calling all townspeople into the streets. One soldier fired a shot, then another. Suddenly, the guards began firing randomly into the mob. The streets erupted into a brawl. Bostonians used any weapon they could find—knives, sticks, and fists—to attack the British soldiers.

Finally, the streets quieted. When the smoke cleared, five Americans were dead. The most well known victim was Crispus Attucks—an African-American sailor and an escaped slave. He was the first man killed in the Revolutionary War. The others were Samuel Gray, James Caldwell, Patrick Carr, and a 17-year-old boy named Samuel Maverick.

If only five people died, why was it called a massacre? American newspapers used the term "massacre" to convince people that British soldiers in the colonies meant trouble. Patriots wanted all Americans to see how dangerous it would be to stay under British rule.

In response to the tea tax, colonists refused to buy tea from the British East India Company. Instead, they bought tea from colonial merchants, who smuggled in the tea from Holland. Soon, the British East India Company had warehouses full of unsold tea. They were in danger of going out of business.

Parliament decided to force the colonists to buy the East India Company's tea. In May 1773, the British government passed the Tea Act. This act allowed the British East India Company to sell tea directly to the colonists at wholesale prices. The colonists could buy tea cheaper than ever before. Parliament thought that the low prices would keep colonists from buying tea from smugglers.

The Tea Act revived the issue of taxation without representation. Even the low prices included a duty tax. If the colonists bought the tea, they would be acknowledging Parliament's right to tax them. Parliament assumed that colonists would rather pay a tax than be without a cup of tea.

The colonists were not so easily fooled. They demanded that the British government remove the tea tax. Dockworkers refused to unload the tea from ships. In turn, the royal governor of Massachusetts, who was

In December 1773, a group of Bostonians boarded three ships of the East India Company and dumped their cargo of tea into the harbor to protest the British policy of taxing tea.

loyal to King George, forced workers to unload the cargo. He also supported the tax.

Finally, Bostonians decided it was time to take action. On December 16, 1773, a group of men disguised themselves as Native Americans and quietly slipped onto the docks of Boston's harbor. They boarded three ships owned by the British East India Company and dumped all of the tea into the ocean. By the end of the night, they had emptied 342 chests of tea, valued at more than 10,000 pounds (almost $19,000). This event became known as the Boston Tea Party.

Parliament responded to the rebels with more laws. British officials passed the Intolerable Acts. One of the acts ordered Boston Harbor to close until the towns-people paid for the destroyed tea. Another act gave more power to the governor of Massachusetts, while eliminating the colony's own legislature. In truth, the governor became a dictator. The colonists no longer had any voice in their own government.

Hale no doubt heard these stories. Like many colonists, he was angry at the way Parliament was treating the colonists. He was eager to get back to the excitement of the city, where he could learn more about what was happening around the colonies.

Test Your Knowledge

I What was the profession of Nathan Hale's father?

   a. Minister.

   b. Farmer.

   c. Lawyer.

   d. Doctor.

2 Why did Deacon Hale name his son Nathan?

   a. Nathan was his own first name.

   b. Nathan was Deacon Hale's father's name.

   c. Nathan was the name of a relative Deacon Hale admired.

   d. None of the above.

3 Who was Alice Adams?

   a. Nathan Hale's stepsister.

   b. Nathan Hale's mother.

   c. Nathan Hale's stepmother.

   d. Nathan Hale's teacher.

4 What college did Nathan Hale attend?

   a. The College of William and Mary.

   b. Harvard College.

   c. Yale College.

   d. He did not attend college.

5 What was Nathan Hale's first job?

a. Spy.

b. Minister.

c. Lawyer.

d. Teacher.

ANSWERS: 1. b; 2. c; 3. a; 4. c; 5. d

Son of
Liberty

In the spring of 1774, Hale finally had the opportunity to leave East Haddam. He accepted a teaching position at the Union Grammar School in New London, Connecticut. Like New Haven, New London was a busy seaport. The city streets buzzed with talk about the increasing numbers of British soldiers in some New England towns.

Townspeople wondered if King George III was worried about a rebellion.

At Union School, Hale taught Latin, literature, mathematics, and writing to about 30 boys. In the morning from 5:00 to 7:00, he also taught a class of young ladies. Hale wanted to make the most out of every hour of the day. Some evenings, he tutored boys after school hours. On his off nights, he conducted science experiments.

Hale was loved and respected by his students and the people of New London. He had grown into a handsome young man—tall and broad, with striking blue eyes and thick, caramel-brown hair. His smooth speech and good humor won him many friends. But his new friends did little to ease his hurting heart.

All of the work in the world could not make Hale forget about his dear Alice. Back home, Alice spent tearful hours alone in her room. Deacon Hale would not back down from his position. He did not want to see his son's promising career held back by boyish love.

Finally, Deacon Hale decided to bring an end to the romance by finding a husband for Alice. Out of her many admirers, he chose Elijah Ripley for her husband. Elijah was a good man and a prosperous Coventry

This one-room schoolhouse where Hale taught has been restored. His students described Hale as a kind, intelligent, popular teacher.

merchant. At that time, a fine young lady would not rebel against her parents' wishes. Alice knew she would never love Elijah, because her heart belonged to Nathan, but she obeyed Deacon Hale's order and agreed to be married.

The news of Alice's upcoming marriage was a bitter blow to Hale. He immediately wrote to his father and begged him to reconsider. He admitted that, while he was not yet ready for a wife, he wanted to marry Alice when he was.

But it was no use. Deacon Hale had made up his mind. In December 1773, Alice and Elijah were married. The union, however, did not last long. A little over a year later, Elijah died. The young widow and her baby returned home.

After her marriage, Alice was no longer considered a child. She was not obligated to obey the deacon's orders. She knew that Nathan Hale was the only man she would ever love. She wrote to him at once and told him everything she felt.

Alice Ripley professed her undying love for Nathan, and he responded in relief and joy. His love for her was true and loyal. But as much as he adored her, Hale frankly told her that they must wait to marry until he was wealthier. Little did he know that far greater obstacles to his marriage would soon appear.

THE PATRIOTS OF NEW LONDON

In 1774, New London was a city of great importance. The coastal seaport was a center of trade between the New England colonies and the colonies to the south. Ships from many nations filled the harbor with imports from distant lands and exports to Europe. The wharves were crowded with rows of warehouses. The merchants of New London had already received letters from Boston urging them not to buy certain items from English ships. The salesmen loyally boycotted all items for the sake of their fellow colonists.

New Londoners held a free and independent spirit. They were a daring and adventurous group of people. Most of the citizens would rather fight than submit to a decision they thought was unjust. The *New London Gazette* was the boldest newspaper in the colonies. It was the first paper to publish the famous speech of Colonel Barre, who called the American patriots "Sons of Liberty." The Sons of Liberty became the name for any group of colonists who worked to rally other Americans against the British.

In December 1774, New Londoners met to discuss the acts of a convention held in Philadelphia on September 5. The convention was in response to the Intolerable Acts of Parliament. Representatives from all colonies except Georgia were present. Samuel Adams and John Adams represented Massachusetts. From Virginia, George Washington and Patrick Henry attended. The representatives voted to cut off all colonial trade with Great Britain until Parliament lifted the Intolerable Acts. They also approved the training of colonists for possible war. This convention later became known as the First Continental Congress. All people at the New London meeting, including Nathan Hale, vowed to stand beside the Sons of Liberty and support the decisions of the First Continental Congress.

The people of New London agreed to stop buying tea. However, some salesmen secretly bought crates of tea from the British East India Company. A council met and asked for the boldest and most patriotic spirits in New London to come forward. Nathan Hale proudly stepped up to help. The group of Patriots seized the tea from the merchants and held a "liberty party" in the city. They burned the crates of tea in a great bonfire. They also gathered all the ribbons and fabric made in Great Britain and threw those items into the fire.

Hale became one of New London's most patriotic residents. He was a favorite with the Patriot leaders. His strong intellect, clear mind, and eloquent speech made him valuable for debates. Hale always knew exactly what to say at the right time.

In 1774, delegates from the colonies gathered in Philadelphia to discuss the response to Britain's Intolerable Acts. The leaders of the First and Second Continental Congresses included men who were closely identified with the cause for independence, such as John Adams, Alexander Hamilton, and Thomas Jefferson.

Patriot meetings were often held at the old, gray stone manor of Nathanial Shaw, a local merchant and trusted friend of George Washington. The men at the manor were interested in the rising tension between the king's officers and their neighboring colony— Massachusetts. There, Hale also met many of the young

(continued on page 38)

Fly a New Flag

Before the American Revolution, the colonies used many different flags. Early designs resembled the British flag, which was the favored flag in the colonies. After war broke out, American regiments each used their own flag designs. When the Patriots declared independence in 1776, George Washington thought that it was important for the Continental Army to unite under a single flag. The design Washington finally chose was a red-and-white-striped banner with 13 stars, one star for each of the 13 colonies. This flag is similar to the one the United States uses today.

When the colonies were first established, settlers flew the British flag. This was the flag of their homeland, or mother country. All American designs descended from this banner. During and after the Revolutionary War, other flags began to appear, including:

The Grand Union Flag. General Washington first chose this flag design in January 1776. The banner looked much like the British flag but with red and white stripes instead of a solid red background.

Don't Tread On Me. Rattlesnake flags were quite popular with the colonists, especially the militant Patriots. Rhode Island naval officer Esek Hopkins used the rattlesnake design for flags that flew on the ships he commanded. The flag boldly stated, "Don't Tread On Me." The phrase emphasized how much the colonists wanted their independence.

Betsy Ross Flag. Some believe that the first flag was created by Betsy Ross, following a design outlined by George Washington. In this design, a circle of 13 five-pointed stars stands on a blue background.

Stars and Stripes Flag. The "Stars and Stripes Flag" was one of the original 13-star flags. It was the most widely used design.

American Stripes. This simple, red-and-white-striped flag was flown on American merchant ships during the Revolutionary War.

Star Spangled Banner. After Vermont and Kentucky joined the Union in the early 1790s, the "Star Spangled Banner" became the official U.S. flag. With 15 stars and 15 stripes, this flag inspired Francis Scott Key to write his famous poem, titled "The Star Spangled Banner." The poem was later put to music and became the national anthem in 1931.

(continued from page 35)

ladies he taught at school in the mornings. He quickly realized that their shyness disappeared outside of the classroom. Many of these bright and energetic women were as dedicated to the cause of liberty as the men. They made it clear that they wanted to be part of the fight for independence. They would be true and endure any danger for the sake of the Patriots.

At one time, British officers delighted in their visits to the port of New London. They shopped at harbor stores, mingled with the charming ladies, and shook hands with friendly men. But the people of New London no longer extended a hand of friendship to the British.

Hale listened intently as the Patriot leaders read letters from other towns. Often, the letters had to be interpreted. Many of them were written in parables only American Patriots could understand. This way, if the letters fell into the hands of British officers, no one would be punished. Some of the men at the meetings brought news from Boston, Philadelphia, or New York. Others reported on what was going on in Virginia. All around the room, stories were exchanged about how the colonies were reacting to the yoke of the British.

The flickering candlelight cast ominous shadows on the faces of the Patriots. Hale and the other young men spoke in low voices. The ladies listened with wide eyes. Everyone wondered what would happen if the king did not relent and agree to colonial demands.

Test Your Knowledge

I In the spring of 1774, Hale left East Haddam and moved where?

    a. New York.

    b. New Haven.

    c. New London.

    d. New Orleans.

2 Which of the following subjects did Hale teach at the Union School?

    a. Latin.

    b. Literature.

    c. Mathematics.

    d. All of the above.

3 After Alice Ripley was widowed, she wanted to marry Hale. Why did he want to postpone the marriage?

    a. He wanted to wait until he had more money.

    b. He wanted to wait until he was settled in New London.

    c. He wanted to wait for his father's blessing.

    d. He was no longer in love with Alice.

4 In New London, Hale served on a council that helped enforce the boycott of what British product?

a. Glass.

b. Tea.

c. Gunpowder.

d. Spices.

5 Hale and his fellow Patriots were concerned by the conflict between British soldiers and citizens of which colony?

a. Connecticut.

b. Pennsylvania.

c. Massachusetts.

d. Virginia.

ANSWERS: 1. c; 2. d; 3. a; 4. b; 5. c

The Shot Heard 'Round the World

Hale was destined to become a soldier. He watched the progress of the militias drilling in New London. Day and night, he wrestled with the decision. He finally came to the conclusion that it was right for every young man to fight for his country. His plan was to resign from teaching when the war came. As soon as there was a call for soldiers, he would go to the battlefront.

Hale was determined to go to war—if war would come—no matter what. This time, even his father could not dissuade him. Much to his joy, both Alice and his brother Richard approved of his decision. His brothers also were eager to help the Sons of Liberty. After all, patriotism ran in the Hale blood. Hale had been named after another Nathan who died fighting for the colonies and England at Louisburg. As a boy, the young schoolmaster had often listened to stories of that Nathan's bravery and death.

In the meantime, Hale attended to his duties as a teacher. The Union School was a model for all others. Hale's discipline was firm but not too harsh. The boys adored their schoolmaster and devoted themselves to learning. Hale showed care to every student, offering special tutoring to those who needed extra help. Hale inspired even the dullest student.

After school, Hale played sports with the boys. Both master and student tried their skills together. Hale showed them how to perform jumps. Thanks to his training, many of the boys became wonderful athletes.

Winter wore away, and spring gave new life to leaders of the liberty movement. The number of British soldiers in the colonies continued to climb, causing colonists to feel as though they were under constant guard. Each passing month brought the climax closer. Patriots in New London boiled with energy. They were ready to jump into service for their country at the first pop of a musket. Only one thing delayed the eruption of violence in the seaport—the fear of the king's men. The British officers felt the patriotic spirit of the town. They did not dare to overstep their authority and give the town a reason to explode.

In early April, the leaders of the revolutionary movement received news from London that King George planned to enforce British rule in the colonies, by whatever means were necessary. Leaders sent messengers to towns in eastern Massachusetts. They scurried about and warned the Patriots to be prepared. On April 13, the Americans formed six artillery companies, in case the British troops attacked.

A RIDE FOR LIBERTY

On April 16, Paul Revere—a dedicated Patriot in Massachusetts—reported to John Hancock and Samuel

Adams in Lexington, on the route from Boston to Concord, warning them that British troops were on their way to arrest the two Patriot leaders. The British troops, or Regulars, had determined to cripple the revolutionary movement by seizing two of its most important leaders. After warning Hancock and Adams, Revere continued on to Concord. There, he instructed Patriots to hide gunpowder and other supplies stored around the town.

On his way back to Boston, Revere stopped in Charlestown. He arranged a signal so that the towns-people would know whether the British troops were coming by land or by sea. Two lanterns were to be placed in the Boston North Church steeple. If one lantern was lit, the British troops were traveling by land. If both lanterns were lit, the Regulars were coming by "sea" over the Charles River.

On the same day that Revere made his ride to Lexington, the British general Thomas Gage received orders from England commanding him to put down the rebellion by arresting its leaders. Gage knew that an arrest of key members in the Massachusetts Provincial Congress—like Hancock and Adams—would drain Patriot manpower. But he decided it was more important to snatch up colonial ammunition stores at Concord. By seizing their powder and weapons, he would reduce the risk of a violent rebellion. Gage planned to march 600 British soldiers from Boston to Lexington on April 19.

Even though he tried to keep it a secret, news of General Gage's plan leaked out. At 10:00 P.M. on the night of April 18, Revere set out on his now famous "midnight ride." First, he told a friend to light the two lanterns in the North Church steeple. The British were marching by sea. Revere headed for Lexington. Along the way, he spotted two British officers. Quickly, Revere steered his horse down another road and just barely slipped away without being noticed. However, he had to take a longer route. All along the road to Lexington, Revere warned the people he encountered that the British Regulars were coming in that direction.

Revere finally reached Lexington after midnight. He rode up to the house where Hancock was staying. The guard outside did not recognize Revere and told him to keep the noise down. "Noise," Paul replied. "You will have noise enough before long. The regulars are coming!"[11] At these words, the guard let him pass. And Revere gave Hancock his report.

American colonists and British soldiers exchanged fire at the Battle of Lexington, the first battle of the Revolutionary War.

THE FIRST SHOTS

Patriot Captain John Parker immediately called together a group of about 70 Minutemen. He told them to be armed and ready to come running when they heard the drum call.

At 4:30 A.M., a Patriot scout ran up to Captain Parker. He reported that the British were less than two miles away. Captain Parker signaled for the drum roll.

The Minutemen hurried to the Lexington Common, ready to fight.

As daylight broke over Lexington, the British Regulars approached the common. The army of Regulars had their muskets loaded, expecting to meet 500 colonial soldiers. Instead, they faced a line of about 40 Minutemen. Another 30 men were scattered around the common and in nearby houses. The British commander, Major Pitcairn, ordered his men to surround and disarm the small militia, but instructed them not to fire.

At the same time, Captain Parker ordered his men to disperse. He did not want his small force in a skirmish with fully armed Regulars. As the Minutemen began to retreat, a single shot rang out. Some people said it came from behind a nearby stone wall. The Regulars immediately sprang into formation and returned fire. Major Pitcairn screamed at his men to stop shooting.

Finally, the shooting died out, and the Regulars marched out of town. When the smoke cleared, seven Lexington Minutemen lay dead in the common. Nine others were wounded. The cries of women and children echoed in the town's streets, and the smell of burnt gunpowder lingered in the air.

Captain Parker ordered the drummers to play. The remaining Minutemen reassembled in the common. The captain calmly informed them that their fellow Patriots in Concord needed their help. The soldiers set off to face the British Regulars again.

Meanwhile, the British marched on to Concord. This time, 500 Minutemen stopped them as they neared the bridge outside of town. Another battle began. Word quickly spread about the fight. Many men rushed to join their fellow Patriots. Finally, they forced the British to retreat to Boston. Many British soldiers were wounded or killed in the battle.

A random shot marked the start of the American Revolution. It later was called "the shot heard 'round the world." The events of April 19 were definitely heard around the colonies. In New London, Hale and other Patriots gathered each night under the shadow of King George's statue. They eagerly awaited the sound of thundering hooves, bringing them news from Massachusetts. Their hearts pounded as they listened to the horrifying tale of Lexington. Still, these men did not dare to breathe a word about independence. But Hale could stand it no longer. It was the mild-mannered schoolteacher who would

The conflict that broke out at Lexington quickly spread to Concord, where colonists and British soldiers clashed in a violent battle.

ring the bell for New London Patriots, and sound the call for freedom.

REVOLUTION HAS COME

On April 20, 1775, the students of Union School all sat at their desks, diligently scribbling on their slates. In the front of the room, Hale was deep into one of his own calculations. A warm, gentle breeze drifted in from an open window. Suddenly, such a commotion broke out in the streets that everyone in the classroom instinctively looked toward the window. The sounds of eager, excited voices created a chatter that grew increasingly louder. The boys turned back and looked questioningly at their teacher.

Curiosity burned deep inside Hale. He had a strange feeling that something dreadfully important had occurred. He wasn't that different from the students in front of him. He, too, wanted to burst through the doors and find out what was happening. However, he stayed calm and kept order.

Several students had popped up from the seats. This one time, they thought that their teacher would bend the rules. "Take your seats, lads," Hale firmly told them. "Finish your lesson."

Disappointed, the boys slumped back to their benches. But the excitement was too much for Hale to bear. He ended class after the first lesson and, within seconds, the students were on the streets. After he closed the schoolhouse doors, Hale's serious manner changed. He laughed as he watched the boys race toward the dense crowd.

"I can give you a good run," he teased one of his students. The two of them raced to the edge of the crowd gathered around King George's statue. It was impossible to push through the crowd. Hale squinted across the heads. The object of everyone's attention was a man on horseback, speaking in a crackling voice.

Who Were the Minutemen?

Today, the terms "militia" and "Minutemen" are sometimes used to mean the same thing. In the eighteenth century, these two groups were quite different. Militia were armed men formed to protect their towns from enemy invasions and raids. The Minutemen were a small, elite fighting force. They were prepared to jump into action at all times. Minutemen were the first armed soldiers to arrive for battle. They were called Minutemen because they had to be ready "in a minute."

Commanders specifically selected their Minutemen. Typically, Minutemen were 25 years old or younger. The commanding officer chose soldiers who were strong, skilled, reliable, and enthusiastic. Although Minutemen are most well known for the Revolutionary War, they had been around since the mid-seventeenth century. By the time of the revolution, the Massachusetts Minutemen had moved into their sixth generation. Minutemen were a well-trained, battle-tested military force. Without them, the Revolutionary War could have had a much different outcome.

Unable to hear what the man was saying, Hale tried to get answers from the people around him. But they just ignored his taps, still straining to catch a scrap of the news. Finally, the man finished speaking, and the crowd let out a great shout.

"I pray you, sir," Hale anxiously asked an old gentleman standing nearby, "tell me what it is all about."

"Haven't you heard?" the man replied. "It is a message from Lexington, where the British have fallen on our brothers and tried to cut them to pieces!"

"It has come, then!" Hale whispered under his breath. "How——," he began, but was cut off.

"Hush, hush, he is going to speak," the man said as he put his hand on Hale's shoulder. He stretched to see over the people. "No, no, he has fallen from his saddle. No wonder, such a ride."

The messenger then sat down on the bench beneath King George. "It is not a good color!" he cried, pointing to the red-coated statue. "That is the emblem of the bloody tyrant!" The crowd answered with loud cheers.

Then a deep voice called out from the middle of the crowd. "Attention friends!" he said. "Let all who wish to help our brave sister, Massachusetts, meet at Miner's Tavern tonight."

"We will all be there!" another man shouted. Many other townspeople nodded their heads in agreement. But others walked away discussing the situation with grave faces. As Hale made his way down the dirt street to his house, he felt as if the one crucial moment in his life had come.[12]

Test Your Knowledge

I How did Hale respond to the growing tension between Britain and the colonies?

　a. He planned to return to his father's farm if war should break out.

　b. He planned to resign his teaching post and volunteer as a soldier if war should break out.

　c. He began to spy on the British, knowing that he could be useful in gathering intelligence.

　d. He urged his fellow Patriots to remain calm and seek a peaceful solution to the conflict.

2 Which two leaders of the rebellion in Massachusetts were British authorities determined to capture?

　a. Paul Revere and John Adams.

　b. Paul Revere and Patrick Henry.

　c. Samuel Adams and John Adams.

　d. Samuel Adams and John Hancock.

3 What signal informed the people of Charlestown how the British troops were traveling?

　a. The sound of approaching gunfire.

　b. The steady sound of troops on the march.

　c. Lanterns hung in the steeple of a church.

　d. The quiet splashing of water against a fleet of boats.

4 Where was the first shot of the Revolutionary
War fired?

   a. Lexington, Massachusetts.

   b. Bunker Hill, Massachusetts.

   c. Saratoga, New York.

   d. Yorktown, Virginia.

5 How did Hale learn of the battles at Lexington
and Concord?

   a. He read about the events in a newspaper.

   b. A messenger arrived in town with the news.

   c. His students informed him.

   d. He could hear the noise of the battles from
his schoolhouse.

ANSWERS: 1. b; 2. d; 3. c; 4. a; 5. b

OUR RIGHTS AND OUR LIBERTIES

For Independence

For many years, Hale had read stories about the
heroes of other times—the generals, captains, and
soldiers whose bravery won them a timeless spot in
history books. Now, important events were happening in
his time—were happening, in fact, all around him. Now
he, too, had the privilege of making a stand for the sake

of freedom and, possibly, performing with courage and bravery.

Hale was realistic enough to know that war was not all about glory and heroism. In the streets of Lexington and Concord, the bodies of young men like him now lay crumpled and lifeless. Not long ago, the colonists first settled America. They faced tremendous hardships, even death, for England. Colonists called England their "mother country." Many Americans still felt a strong bond between their new country and their homeland. But this spilling of blood had forever divided them.

At Miner's Tavern that night, tongues found it difficult to keep quiet. Women whispered in the corners. Men raised their voices in heated discussions and pounded their fists on the tables. Hale calmly stood up and walked through the crowd. The noisy crowd hushed as he stepped onto the platform. The 20-year-old schoolteacher spoke with more passion and eloquence than ever before. Throughout the room, tears ran down the cheeks of many listeners.

"Let us not lay down our arms till we have gained independence!" he said.[13] He had spoken the word that everyone had been thinking but no one dared to utter—independence. Inspired, they responded to the schoolteacher's passionate words.

"Independence!" they cried back.

As Hale stepped down, the room burst into loud claps and cheers. Men and women jumped to their feet to give him a standing ovation. They shook his hand or patted him on the back as he walked by.

On May 10, 1775, a Second Continental Congress met in Philadelphia. Members elected John Hancock as the president. At this meeting, an American army was established—the Continental Army. The Congress chose George Washington to lead the American forces.

At that time, America did not have a draft system. The Continental Army relied on volunteer soldiers. Most colonists were farmers, not experienced military men. The soldiers agreed to join for one year of service. Minutemen served for only a few months. By July 1775, about 17,000 men had joined the Continental Army. But because the volunteers had farms or businesses to run, and families to support, it was a struggle to keep soldiers from leaving after their year was up. By December 1775, the army had dwindled to fewer than 6,000 soldiers.

In 1775, the Second Continental Congress selected Virginian
George Washington to lead the Continental Army. He quickly
traveled to Massachusetts to take command of the troops.

King George III was not too worried about the Continental Army. Great Britain had a large, well-trained, professional army. However, British generals soon found that British fighting methods did not always work in the colonies. In Europe, Regulars fought on wide, open fields. Many Revolutionary War battles took place in tighter areas. The British realized that they would not have the quick and easy victory they had originally expected.

CAPTAIN HALE

As Hale left Miner's Tavern, his future course was clear. The war had come at last, and he must fulfill his duty. He immediately asked for a spot in the New London militia, which was leaving for Massachusetts the next morning. At daybreak, the soldiers began their march.

Hale trained with the army for several months and then, in early July, he returned home for a few days. He accepted a full-time spot in the New London Company and resigned from his teaching position.

On July 7, he sat down at his writing desk and opened a jar of ink. He carefully dipped a feather quill in the jar and began writing a letter to the school.

"Gentlemen," he wrote, "Having received information that a place is allotted to me in the army, and being inclined as I hope, for good reasons, to accept it, I am constrained to ask . . . to be excused from keeping your school any longer." Regretfully, he continued, "School-keeping is a business of which I was always fond . . . but at present there seems an opportunity for more extended public service."[14] When he resigned, one townsperson remembered how sincerely he cared about the future of his students. "He gave them council, prayed with them, shook each by the hand," before saying good-bye.[15]

In mid-July, Hale joined the Connecticut army as a lieutenant under the command of Major John Latimer. From August through September, the army stayed in New London to defend the port from British attacks. Hale's exceptional discipline and dedication earned him a promotion. On September 1, he became captain of his own company—the Nineteenth Continental Regiment.

On September 24, General George Washington ordered all Connecticut troops to report to him in Boston. From September 28, 1775, through April 1776, the troops all camped in and around Boston. Hale exercised and trained his company so well that his men stood out above other soldiers. General Washington personally complimented Hale on the admirable skill of his men.

In those days, soldiers often left the army when they became tired or sick. When Hale's men were anxious to return home, he pleaded with them to stay. He spoke with such smooth and inspiring words that the soldiers turned around and unpacked their sacks. Hale generously divided up all of his own army pay and gave it to the men. He sacrificed personal items and private supplies just to keep his company together. His men eventually transformed into hardened, strong soldiers. Despite the hardships, none of his company murmured a complaint. They were always ready to take on the greatest of dangers.

Hale was faithful to his military duties, but also took time to build friendships with his men. At night, he sometimes played cards with the soldiers. In a diary entry dated November 8, 1775, Hale wrote, "Cleaned my gun—played some football, and some checkers."[16] If his men became sick, Hale visited them and prayed with them. Very few captains were as devoted to their men as Hale was.

During the winter of 1775, Hale was granted a temporary leave and returned to Coventry. He was overjoyed to once again see his beloved Alice. But the reunion was short-lived. Soon, he was on the march back to Boston. Along the way, he stopped in New Haven to visit a close friend. After Hale left, his friend's father said, "That man is a diamond of the first water, calculated to excel in any station he assumes. He is a gentleman and a scholar, and last though not least, of his qualifications, a Christian."[17]

The Continental Army had its first major victory at Dorchester Heights near Boston. On March 4, 1776, Patriot troops marched up the hills overlooking Boston Harbor. They began firing cannons at the British troops below. The British retreated out of Boston to their ships and sailed out of the port. The Americans had control of Boston.

After this victory, the colonies officially declared their independence from Great Britain. Thomas Jefferson wrote the Declaration of Independence, and the Continental Congress approved it on July 4, 1776. The 13 colonies considered themselves free states.

In July 1776, British General Howe anchored his ships off Long Island, New York. More than 30,000

British soldiers prepared to capture New York City. Their orders were to break up the rebel colonists and put an end to the revolution.

Hale's company marched to join the Continental Army in New York. The diligence and military skill of his company became the envy of all the officers. Other captains came to Hale for advice. General Washington took a special interest in the young captain, who stood out as a brave and daring Patriot.

STEALING A SLOOP

Hale's enthusiasm rubbed off on his company. He had drilled them, pushed them, and inspired them to stay. Over the months, the soldiers grew to love and respect their captain. When the opportunity for a dangerous mission came about, Hale's men were as eager as their brave commander to engage in it.

A British war ship, the *Asia*, was anchored in the East River of New York. The ship guarded a smaller supply sloop. Hale carefully eyed both vessels from every approach—on land and on water. He decided that this mission was risky, but could be accomplished. Hale was determined to steal the sloop from under the great ship.

Hale demonstrated bravery and boldness during one of his earliest missions—to steal a British supply ship that was anchored in the East River of New York (shown here as it appeared in 1776).

Such a hazardous mission could only be carried out by cool and daring men. Hale dared not mention his plan to the other officers. He knew that they would refuse to let him take the risk. Instead, Hale secretly recruited some of his own men for the task.

Just before the moon rose, Hale and his men met on the riverbank. They boarded a tiny skiff and pushed off. The water was so calm that the boat barely made a ripple. The enemy was completely unaware of their crossing.

They landed on the opposite shore and crept down to a spot near the sloop. They waited and watched in silence until Hale chose the right moment to make their move. The men knew that the littlest noise would mean discovery and certain death.

In the early morning hours, the moon disappeared, and a heavy darkness fell over the river. At last, the time had come. The crew hurried back to the skiff and rowed out to the sloop. On board the *Asia*, all was quiet. The only sound they heard was the monotonous cry of the night guard: "All's well!"[18]

The Patriots made it to the bow of the sloop. The next minute, they were over the side and on the deck. Hale seized the steering wheel, or helm, and pointed the ship toward the American camp. The others kept watch over the *Asia*. On the war ship, the British sailors were still undisturbed in their bunks. As the sloop drifted into the camp wharf, Hale could still hear a faint call from the British ship: "All's well!"

Hale and his brave men gave three loud cheers. "Huzzah, huzzah, huzzah!" they shouted.[19] (Huzzah was a colonial way of saying "hurrah.") Soon, other

American soldiers joined Hale's men on the dock. The sloop was a great steal. It was rich with food, clothing, and other supplies.

Around camp, Hale was treated like a hero. In those days, it wasn't easy to raise the spirits of the soldiers. The army had dwindled with sickness and hunger. But Hale was now able to give his men some money, and offer them food and clothing—both of which were in short supply. Soldiers who had been frightened and depressed were smiling with delight. They owed it all to their fearless leader, Captain Hale.

Hale's boldness captured the attention of Colonel Thomas Knowlton. The colonel had formed a group of men known as Knowlton's Rangers. The Rangers patrolled the shorelines along the island of Manhattan in New York. After Hale's daring mission on the East River, Knowlton invited the captain to join his elite group of soldiers.

Test Your Knowledge

I Who was elected president of the Second
   Continental Congress?
   a. George Washington.
   b. John Adams.
   c. John Hancock.
   d. Benjamin Franklin.

2 George Washington was chosen to command a new,
   unified American army. What was its name?
   a. The Minutemen.
   b. The Continental Army.
   c. The Union Army.
   d. The Army of the United States.

3 Hale became a captain in the army of which colony?
   a. New York.
   b. Virginia.
   c. Connecticut.
   d. Massachusetts.

4 Washington's troops had their first major victory
   near which city?
   a. Boston.
   b. New London.
   c. New York.
   d. Philadelphia.

5 Hale and his men accepted a dangerous mission
to steal what?

a. A supply ship.

b. A war ship.

c. A cannon.

d. A British regiment's gunpowder.

A Spy!

General Howe made an outstanding march into New York. During the Battle of Long Island, he captured thousands of Patriots and threw them into the British military jail, or provost jail, in New York City. Washington's troops were forced to make a panicked retreat. Without a full-proof strategy, hopes for taking back New York looked bleak.

General Washington paced back and forth in his tent. His next move against the British had to be planned with the greatest care. His army had no stores or defenses to fall back on, and the British seemed to have an endless supply of men and equipment. In order to make a successful attack, he would need to anticipate General Howe's plans.

Washington knew that the British commander was experienced and capable. At that very moment, he was probably preparing to advance and close in on the Continental Army, bringing the Americans to a crushing defeat.

The American general needed information of the strictest kind. This intelligence could only come from inside the enemy lines. Washington needed a spy. To take the name of a spy was a disgraceful thing, even under honorable circumstances. Usually, a spy or traitor was associated with greed and revenge. A spy also had a dangerous job. If the traitor was discovered, he would be sentenced to death by hanging.

Sending out a spy was Washington's last resort. But he was desperate. In order to surround and defeat the British, he needed to know their weaknesses.

This spy would need incredible qualifications. The hazardous task required an educated man, familiar with land drawings and army movements. He would need to identify and uncover British fortifications, or strong spots. The spy must mingle with British officers, create false friendships, and obtain classified information. The job called for a man of great bravery and trustworthiness.

General Washington asked Colonel Knowlton to call together his Rangers. Knowlton frankly asked for a volunteer. There was a long moment of silence. The men looked at each other, not wondering who would respond, but in shock that the colonel would ask such a thing. Some faces turned from confused to angry. They were noble fighters, not treacherous spies.

The colonel saw the looks on their faces. "This duty would greatly serve the American army," he explained. "Your general is distressed. Without this information, our country is in great danger. Our armies would suffer terrible defeat, and many lives will be lost."

While Knowlton was speaking, Hale stepped forward. He looked around the room and wondered why no man was willing to do what his country needed most.

"I will undertake it," he answered.

Faces turned in shock. "Captain Hale!" exclaimed his good friend, General Hull. "You do not know what you are saying. You—a spy?"[20]

"It is out of the question," cried several others. "There must be someone else."

"Who?" Hale asked, knowing that no other man would volunteer. The men all looked down at the ground.

Even Colonel Knowlton hated to see the proud young captain take on such a role. He tried to get a French sergeant to accept the task instead. The sergeant replied, "I am willing to fight like a man for the republic. I will not let myself die the death of a dog."

Hale's friends grabbed him by the coat and begged him not to do it. Hale shook himself free. "I think I owe to my country [a task] so important and so much desired by the commander of her armies," he said. "I know no other mode of obtaining the information than by assuming a disguise and passing into the enemy's camp." He took a deep breath and stood tall. "I am fully sensible of the consequences of discovery and capture in such a situation."[21]

A Spy!

75

The friends who hoped to change his mind found themselves inspired instead. Before them, they saw the vision of a brave hero, not a traitor. With tearful eyes, they wished him luck and prayed for his safety.

BEHIND ENEMY LINES

Whatever Washington wanted him to do, Hale would meet it with force and determination. He knew that the general cared for him and would probably try to dissuade him from taking the assignment when they were alone. But Hale held firm.

No one knows for sure what words were spoken between the captain and general during the long interview. Washington probably put aside his feelings as a general and, as Hale's friend, warned him of the dangers that lay ahead. And Hale certainly answered with firmness and vowed to do what his country required.

By the middle of September, Hale was ready to go. He told his servant, Asher Wright, to watch over his things. He asked Asher to take the items along if the army moved on.

Asher agreed and took tender care of Hale's diary, books, and camp belongings. At times, he lagged

Hale gave up the proud uniform of a Continental soldier to don the plain brown suit he wore as a disguise while serving as a spy.

behind the army because he had to gather these items together. He later said that he would rather be captured by the British than leave them behind. At the time, Asher did not know where Hale was going. When he found out, he said, "He was too good-looking to go so. He could not deceive. Some scrubby fellows ought to have gone."[22]

Armed with all the necessary items, Hale left the army and walked from Harlem Heights to Norwalk— 50 miles up the Connecticut shore. His journey along the coast was uneventful. As he walked, he looked for a way to get across the East River to the British side. But the waters were cluttered with British vessels on the lookout for American boats.

At Norwalk, Hale found a ship that would take him across the river. He disguised himself as a traveling schoolmaster, in a plain brown suit and a round, wide-brimmed hat. It was the character he felt most comfortable playing. He left his uniform and papers with a friend but kept his diploma and watch. These two items would make his schoolmaster character believable.

That night, he boarded the sloop and made passage across the river. He landed in a place called The Cedars.

He arranged to have the boat come daily to the same spot, knowing that one day soon, he would be back. Hale walked through a settlement of Loyalists—those Americans loyal to the British crown. He continued all the way to New York City. The British had greatly advanced into the city since Hale had left Harlem Heights. Much of Long Island was occupied by the enemy, from Red Hook to Flushing Bay and from Brooklyn deep into the island.

The British cavalry patrolled the streets daily. They were not as hateful toward the Patriots as the Loyalists, whose only goal was to capture American stragglers and turn them in to the British. But Hale still had to be alert and calm at all times. With his pleasant manner and good humor, he quickly made friends with British officers and soldiers. He would utter phrases designed to reassure the British of his Loyalist sympathies, going so far as to call on King George to protect him from the rebel Patriots.

Before long, Hale made it to the heart of the enemy. He wandered through the camps, joking with officers and soldiers. The proud soldiers were more than happy to tell him how prepared they were to destroy the American troops. All the while, Hale paid careful attention to the fortifications, carrying images of the plans in his mind. He sat up late into the night, sketching the posts.

Day after day, he passed by jails of sickly Patriot prisoners. He watched the British carry out dead soldiers or march them away to be executed. It must have deeply pained Hale to watch his fellow Patriots suffering and be unable to save them.

After several weeks, Hale was satisfied with all the information he had gathered. He had all the details necessary for General Washington to execute an attack that would break the British and place New York in American hands. He did not want to waste any time. He worried that the Patriots might make a move before he returned. Hale folded up the precious documents containing the British plans and slid them into his

(continued on page 82)

Spy Letters in Invisible Ink

Both the Continental Army and the British Army wrote secret letters in invisible ink. The invisible message was written between the lines of an ordinary letter. If the letter was intercepted by the enemy, the message would look like a regular letter.

At the time of the Revolutionary War, invisible ink was made from a mixture of ferrous sulfate and water. Invisible messages could be read in one of two ways. The reader would either heat the letter by holding it over a candle flame, or brush the letter with the chemical sodium carbonate. British spies marked the letter with an F for fire or an A for acid to let the reader know how to treat it.

Letters written with invisible ink needed special care. If the paper got wet, the ink could easily smear. The smeared ink would make the message impossible to read. Spies made sure to keep their letters in a safe and dry spot, such as in a coat pocket or carrying bag.

Patriots frequently used invisible ink to send messages to General Washington. Examples of these letters are kept at the Library of Congress in a special section of Washington's papers. The British wrote invisible letters less often than the Americans. But a letter written by Loyalist Benjamin Thompson still exists. Thompson was the earliest and most famous scientist in colonial America. The letter looks dark brown, probably from being heated over a flame.

WRITE AN INVISIBLE MESSAGE
You can create invisible ink with the help of an adult.

You Will Need:

    Small saucepan   Toothpicks

    Water   Paper

    Cornstarch   Small bowl

    Spoon   Iodine

    Stove top or hotplate   Sponge

Make Invisible Ink:

1. In the saucepan, mix 4 teaspoons of water with 2 tablespoons of cornstarch. Stir until smooth.

2. Stirring constantly, heat the mixture over a stove burner or a hotplate (remember to get an adult's permission or help) for several minutes or until it thickens.

3. Dip a toothpick into the mixture and write a message on a piece of paper. Re-dip the toothpick in the "ink" if the tip runs dry.

4. Set the paper aside, and let it dry.

5. Meanwhile, mix one teaspoon of iodine and 10 teaspoons of water in a small bowl.

6. When the paper is dry, dip the tip of a sponge into the iodine solution. Carefully wipe the paper. The message should turn purple.

(continued from page 79)

shoes. With padded feet, he began the homeward journey at once.

Hale traveled safely through the British outskirts and hostile Loyalist territory. Finally, he was back at The Cedars on September 21. It was early morning, and his boat was not there to meet him. So Hale decided to stop at a nearby Loyalist tavern for a bite to eat. He was sure that no one would recognize him in his clever disguise.

Hale sat down at a table and ordered breakfast. He struck up a conversation with some of the Loyalists there. One man in the corner seemed familiar to him. But Hale was so entertained by the discussion that he did not notice the man slip out.

Several hours passed. Hale thought that he should go to watch for his boat. The waitress cleared the table and glanced out the window. "There's a strange boat coming ashore," she announced.

The Loyalists quickly scattered, fearing a Patriot attack. They begged Hale to come with them. "If they are rebels," Hale replied, "Surely they will not hassle a poor schoolmaster."

Hale quickly left the tavern, confident that it was the boat for which he had been waiting. He ran down to the shore. Suddenly, a dozen men popped up with their muskets aimed at Hale. "Surrender or die!" they yelled.[23]

BETRAYED

Hale had been betrayed! His mind jumped back to the tavern and that familiar face on the man who had slipped away. Hale looked around. Loyalists quickly surrounded him on all sides. There was no escape. If he tried to make a run for it, he would certainly be shot. Life was dear to him, so he clung to the slim chance that he could somehow escape his captors later.

British soldiers led Hale onto the boat. Among the crew, Hale saw the man from the tavern. Their eyes met, and Hale suddenly remembered who he was. The informer was none other than his own cousin, Samuel Hale. Samuel was the son of Nathan's uncle—Richard's brother. Hale thought about how disappointed his father would be, and what a disgrace Samuel had brought on the family.

Soldiers rowed the prisoner to the guard ship— the *Halifax*. Captain Quarme received Hale with courtesy, but sternness.

"State your name," the captain ordered.

"Nathan Hale." He did not try to deny it.

"Are you a captain in the Continental Army?" Quarme asked.

"I am," Hale calmly replied.

"Where is your uniform?" the British captain inquired. "Why are you dressed as a schoolteacher, Captain?" Hale refused to answer.[24]

Quarme ordered his men to search the prisoner. The British soldiers fingered through Hale's pockets and sleeves. They lifted the hat off his head and looked inside. They found nothing.

Then, they looked down at his feet. "Remove your shoes," the captain told him. In the soles, the soldiers found the plans and maps Hale was going to give Washington. All hope of release vanished. The truth was exposed—he was a traitor. The *Halifax* would take him back to New York.

Even though Hale was a spy, his bravery, dignity, and calm attitude won the respect of Captain Quarme. Most spies were treated with scorn, but the British captain later regretted "that so fine a fellow had fallen into his powers."[25] Nevertheless, the captain's duty required him to be true to his British superiors.

As Hale was being led to the docks, New York was ablaze. The 21-year-old prisoner was led through the chaos, as people threw their belongings out windows and British Redcoats chased suspected arsonists.

Hale would have held on to the hope that he could escape or, perhaps, be rescued in New York. What he did not know was that New York was facing a crisis at that very moment. The city had been on fire since 2:00 A.M. Both sides of Broadway, stretching along the city, were a mass of flames and smoke. The lower part of the city swarmed with soldiers who were trying to battle the blaze. Terrified citizens ran about grabbing any property they could save. No one took any interest in the 21-year-old prisoner being led along the docks. The fire continued devouring the streets until 493 houses and one-third of the city were reduced to ashes.

Hale soon realized that he would find no one to save him from his fate. He held his chin firm and focused his eyes straight ahead. He followed the British soldiers as they led him to the quarters of General Howe.

Test Your Knowledge

1 Why were there no other volunteers for the spying mission?

   a. Spying was viewed as dishonorable.

   b. The soldiers had lost confidence in Washington's leadership.

   c. The soldiers were exhausted from fighting and wanted to return home.

   d. Hale had the most experience in spying and was the obvious choice for the mission.

2 What two items did Hale carry to make his disguise believable?

   a. A book and a ruler.

   b. A globe and a notebook.

   c. A diploma and a watch.

   d. A dictionary and a quill pen.

3 Hale spied on British troops stationed where?

   a. Boston.

   b. Philadelphia.

   c. Providence.

   d. Long Island.

4 Where did Hale hide the secret documents he was carrying?

    a. In his hat.

    b. In his shoes.

    c. In his pocket.

    d. In a saddlebag.

5 Who betrayed Nathan Hale?

    a. The owner of the tavern.

    b. A suspicious British soldier.

    c. A soldier in the Continental Army.

    d. Hale's cousin, Samuel Hale.

ANSWERS: 1. a; 2. c; 3. d; 4. b; 5. d

But
One Life

Three miles from New York's City Hall was a mansion built by devoted Patriot James Beckman. As the British moved into the city, Beckman abandoned his house. The mansion was spacious and stately. General Howe selected it for his headquarters. The Beckman house was close to the center of the city and far enough away from the military jail.

The commander would not be disturbed by unpleasant sounds from the prison.

Hale met General Howe in the mansion greenhouse. Howe's appearance reminded the young captain of General Washington. He was tall, slender, dignified, and walked with majestic loftiness. But, unlike Washington, his face was harsh. He had a quick and fierce temper. Howe was already in a foul mood. He was tired from a long day's work, irritated by the fire that had destroyed much of the city, and extremely hungry. The news of an American spy did not sweeten his attitude.

General Howe had a reputation for being a just man. However, nothing roused the anger of officers more than a spy. Still, when the general saw this nice-looking young man standing before him, he had to ask the officers to repeat the charge. "He's an American spy, Sir," they answered.[26]

Howe frowned and took a seat behind his desk. He began questioning Hale about his business. Hale answered with direct and calm responses. He did not try to hide his work or purpose. Howe studied the drawings. The papers included every one of the commander's plans. His carefully built fortifications were sketched

Once he was unmasked as a spy, Hale was brought before
General Howe, the commander of the British Army in America.

and described in incredible detail. Howe was amazed at how successfully this spy had completed his job.

Hale did not ask for a trial by court martial. He knew what the sentence was for a spy. But he did defend himself when General Howe asked him why a man of his learning would reduce himself to a spy.

"I am serving my country," Hale flatly replied. "Any service she needs, I will perform."[27]

Inwardly, Howe admired Hale's ambition. "What a gain this would be to turn him to our side," he thought.[28] He offered Hale a full pardon if he would join the British Army.

Hale refused to purchase his life at the price of his country. "Nothing makes me more loyal to my country than a temptation to forsake her," he said.[29]

"Then you may die for her," Howe grimly declared.[30]

He turned to William Cunningham, the provost marshal of the royal army. "Take Nathan Hale into your custody," he ordered. "Keep him guarded until morning. At daybreak, he will be hung by the neck until dead."[31]

A FEW HOURS BEFORE DAYBREAK

The young captain had served his country. But the priceless information would never reach General

Washington. And the Continental Army was about to lose a gallant soldier. Hale listed to his sentence without saying a word. He gave no sign of agony. At a slight touch from the guard, Hale willingly turned around and followed the soldiers to the prison.

The news of Hale's capture had quickly spread throughout the British Army. As he walked through the streets, a crowd of officers and soldiers gathered to get a peek at the masterful spy.

The guards took Hale to the prison. He was in William Cunningham's custody. Hale had heard many stories about this man's brutality. He calmly studied the ruthless guard. Cunningham was a large, bulky man with a ruddy complexion. In his earlier years, Cunningham served as a soldier in the British Dragoons—a unit of the cavalry. He came to New York, where he joined the Loyalists, and was eager to perform any cruel task to torture the Patriots.

Cunningham hated liberty and did his best to punish those who fought for it. He cheated the prisoners' rations, kicked them, beat them, and insulted them. At all times, he carried a coiled rope on his arm. He randomly chose men to hang and left their bodies dangling in the jail yard to scare the other prisoners.

(continued on page 96)

Spy Codes and Ciphers

American spies carried messages between generals, Patriot leaders, and other prominent members of the Revolution. There was always a chance that these notes might be intercepted by British soldiers. Therefore, it was important that the messages were written in secret codes.

The most common code was an alphanumeric substitution system. In this system, the letters A to Z were replaced with a number from 1 to 26. Because this code was a standard practice, some Patriots worried that the messages would be easily decoded. They developed new codes and ciphers, or decoding keys.

In 1775, Charles Dumas designed the first diplomatic cipher to be used by the Continental Congress and Benjamin Franklin. Patriots used the cipher to communicate with agents and allies in Europe. Leaders selected a paragraph of French literature as the cipher. Dumas's system substituted numbers for letters in the order they appeared within the paragraph. This method was more secure than the standard alphanumeric system, because each letter of plain text could be replaced with more than one number. In other words, it was trickier for the British to decode.

Another system was created by Hale's college friend Benjamin Tallmadge—a member of the Culper spy ring.

This network of spies passed secret messages from New York City to George Washington in upstate New York. The ring was so secret that General Washington did not even know who the members were. Spies included Robert Townsend, Aaron Woodhull, Austin Roe, Anna Strong, and Caleb Brewster. The group worked through a system of package deliveries for the code name "Samuel Culper."

The Culper spy ring used a numerical substitution code drawn up by Tallmadge. Tallmadge selected several hundred words from a dictionary and several dozen names of people and places. He assigned a number for each of them—from 1 to 763. For example, 38 meant attack, 192 stood for fort, George Washington was number 711, and New York was 727. An American agent disguised as a deliveryman would carry the message packages to other members of the ring. Anna Strong would signal the package's location through a code with her laundry. A black petticoat hung out on the line meant that the message was ready to be picked up. The number of handkerchiefs on the line would indicate the location of the cove on Long Island Sound where the spies should meet. The elaborate scheme was incredibly successful.

(continued from page 93)

The provost jail held the most wretched prisoners. It was heavily guarded on all sides. The food was horrible, the cells were overcrowded, and in the damp air hung a vile stench. This place was hardly suitable for the final hours of a great hero.

But Hale's heart was far away. A short time stood between him and eternity. For a moment, he must have forgotten where he was as thoughts of his dear Alice flooded into his mind. It would take every last minute just to write his goodbyes to Alice and his father. He also wanted to give his love to each of his brothers and sisters, nephews, and close friends. He needed to tell them he met his fate as a true soldier and Patriot. His only regret was that he could not serve his country longer.

Cunningham pushed Hale into his cell. Hale held up his chained wrists. "Would you unlock my hands?" he asked. "So I may write letters to my friends." Cunningham pretended to ignore him and slammed the door shut.

If he could not write his goodbyes, then Hale wanted to prepare himself for what was to come. "May I have a Bible?" he asked Cunningham.

"Why do you need a book to make your repentance?" Cunningham laughed.

A young guard standing nearby had sympathy for Hale. He was brave enough to stand up to Cunningham. "Give the man his requests," he demanded.[32]

Surprisingly, Cunningham backed down and shuffled off to take his anger out on someone else. The young guard moved Hale to a lit cell where he could write his letters in peace. Somehow, Hale found the courage to give his loved ones words of strength. He spent the dark hours forgetting about his fate and comforting others.

SWING THE REBEL OFF!

Morning came too soon on September 22, 1776. When Cunningham came into Hale's cell, he found the captain ready and waiting for his punishment. Hale had never touched the oak plank that was his bed. He had no thought of sleep during those last few hours of his life.

Hale handed his letters to Cunningham. He searched the marshal's face for some sign of trustworthiness. He wanted to believe that Cunningham would at least fulfill the request of a dying man.

But Cunningham responded with the unthinkable. He tore open the letters and quickly skimmed the pages in search of some sorrow or weakness. The marshal found no cowardly words, only noble and patriotic feelings. He tore the letters into pieces and let them drop to the dusty floor.

A new type of torture pained Hale's suffering soul. All the careful writing he had done in his final hours was left in shreds to be trampled by the British. Hale was helpless. There was no friend in sight of whom to ask a favor. No one could take a parting message to his family.

It must have taken every bit of strength to keep from lunging at the unfeeling marshal. Hale probably wanted to shout hateful insults at the man who was tearing at his very soul. Instead, Hale took a deep breath and collected his emotions. He was determined to spend his final moments peacefully, not in rage and revenge.

The morning sun hit Hale's face as he stepped into the jail yard. "Prepare for your death march," Cunningham jeered.[33] A large tree stood in the center of the square. From one of the branches, a rope dangled and swayed in the wind. Beneath the tree, a grave had already been dug for his body, a sight that would surely shake the strongest heart.

The town learned that Cunningham was about to string up another victim, and a crowd gathered in the yard. The people pitied Hale and let out cries when they saw such a young and handsome man awaiting this terrible death. Their wails grew so loud that Cunningham had to order them to be silent.

Hale stood behind the hanging tree, his hands tied behind his back. He wore a white jacket, white overalls, and a white cap over his shiny brown hair. The crowd gathered to witness Hale's hanging saw a man standing tall and proud. On his face, he wore a look of confidence and great purpose.

The hangman kicked Hale's coffin directly below the noose and ordered him to climb the ladder. Cunningham watched the brave captain climb up the ladder without the slightest quiver. He wanted to see the Patriot crumble, cry, and beg for mercy. The marshal thought he had one last chance to break Hale. "Speak your final words," he shouted.[34]

Hale's eyes scanned past the crowd. He must have tried to absorb all of the beauty of the world in those final breaths. These images would be the last things he would see and hear. He gazed at the orange streaks of

Hale did not falter as he was led to his execution, demonstrating bravery and conviction in his final hours.

sunlight spreading across the sky. The smoky haze hanging over the city made it all seem like a dream.

Even though much of the city lay in ruins, the colonists would soon rebuild it. The strength to overcome hardship was in the American blood. And although he had not completed his mission, Hale had not failed. The Patriots would find a way to overcome.

With a strong and steady voice, Hale spoke. He said, "I only regret that I have but one life to lose for my country."[35]

The provost marshal was stunned by Hale's unshakable courage. The Patriot's last words were noble, not cowardly. Cunningham's rage boiled.

"Swing the rebel off!" he growled.[36]

Test Your Knowledge

I Once captured, Hale was brought before which
British general?

   a. General Lafayette.

   b. General Howe.

   c. General Darrow.

   d. General Manchester.

2 The British general offered Hale a full pardon
if he would agree to do what?

   a. Join the British Army.

   b. Spy on General Washington.

   c. Provide details of Continental Army
fortifications.

   d. Give up the names of other Patriot spies.

3 What two requests did Hale make of the prison
warden?

   a. He asked for a pen and paper.

   b. He asked him to send a message to General
Washington and to his father, informing
them of his capture.

   c. He asked for a chance to see his father
and Alice one last time.

   d. He asked for a Bible and for his hands
to be unlocked.

4 What happened when Hale handed his letters to William Cunningham?

    a. Cunningham agreed to make sure that they were delivered.

    b. Cunningham returned the letters, explaining that prisoners could not send mail.

    c. Cunningham tore up the letters.

    d. Cunningham gave the letters to the British general.

5 What were Hale's final words?

    a. "Give me liberty or give me death!"

    b. "I only regret that I have but one life to lose for my country."

    c. "These are the times that try men's souls."

    d. "I have only begun to fight!"

ANSWERS: 1. b; 2. a; 3. d; 4. c; 5. b

A New Nation

News about Hale's capture and death did not reach the Patriots right away. After a spy was executed, the body was left hanging as an example and warning to others. Eventually, someone recognized the dead man as Hale, and the news spread by word of mouth.

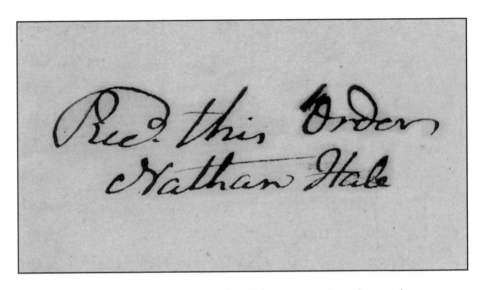

Hale's final letters to his family did not survive, but other mementos of his service did. This acceptance of an order contains the signature of Continental Army officer Nathan Hale.

On November 30, Hale's brother Enoch heard a rumor of Nathan's death. He wrote in his diary, "Heard a rumor that Captain Hale . . . was seen to hang on the enemies lines at New York being taken as a spy . . . hope it is without foundation—something troubled [me and I did not sleep very well]."[37]

A few days later, Enoch heard more rumors, very similar to the first. He began to fear the worst. He received official word of Nathan's execution on October 26.

After Hale's death, the outlook for American forces was grim. They continued to suffer defeats at the hand of the British. On December 26, 1776, General Washington marched his troops through a snowstorm toward Trenton, New Jersey. The soldiers boarded boats and rowed across the Delaware River. They took the Hessian forces (who were hired by the British to fight on their side) by surprise. Many of the enemy soldiers were still asleep. After a brief battle, the Patriots captured nearly 900 soldiers.

This amazing victory fueled Patriot support. Many more men enlisted in the Continental Army. The revolution once again began building momentum. The Americans won another victory at Saratoga, New York in October 1777. There, British General John Burgoyne surrendered his entire army of 5,700 men.

The Battle of Saratoga convinced France that the Patriots could win the war. In February 1778, France agreed to help the Americans fight the British. The French hoped to win back some of the land they had lost to the British during the French and Indian War. Later, Spain and Holland also joined the Patriots in their struggle against Great Britain.

FINAL BATTLES

After 1779, fighting began in the southern colonies. In the south, the British won many of the battles. They quickly took control of Georgia. In 1780, British soldiers captured Charleston, South Carolina. During the attack, Regulars took more than 5,000 colonists as prisoners.

In March 1781, American troops met the British near Greensboro, North Carolina. They fought the Battle of Guilford Courthouse. Patriots forced the enemy to retreat. After several small battles, American troops pushed the British out of North Carolina. The Regulars had to retreat to either Charleston, South Carolina, or Savannah, Georgia. After these battles, the Continental Army controlled the rest of the South.

Not all colonists supported the American army. Almost 80,000 people left the colonies after the Declaration of Independence was approved. Many Southerners stayed to fight the Patriots as Loyalists. In October 1780, the Loyalists fought the Patriots at the Battle of King's Mountain in South Carolina. The Patriots won an overwhelming victory. They killed 150 Loyalists and captured 600 others. This win helped bring an end to Loyalist support in the colonies.

The Hale family home in Coventry is shown in this photo.
Hale did not live here; the building was completed a
month after Hale's execution.

The final battle of the war began in September 1781 at Yorktown, Virginia. Yorktown was a thriving port. There, British General Cornwallis and an army of 7,000 soldiers waited for a supply ship. General Washington learned that a French sailing fleet was on its way to North America. He decided to combine French and Patriot forces in an attack on Yorktown.

The American forces trapped the British Army. The French fleet barricaded the port so that no supplies could arrive by sea. On land, the Continental Army and French troops kept the British from retreating out of the town. On October 17, 1781, Cornwallis surrendered. King George III was not ready to end the war, but Parliament decided it would cost them too much money to continue fighting.

On September 3, 1783, American and British leaders signed the Treaty of Paris, bringing an end to the Revolutionary War. The 13 colonies had gained independence. They named their new country the United States of America. In September 1788, the U.S. government approved the Constitution. George Washington was elected the first president of the United States.

In 1793, ten years after the Treaty of Paris, an old man put up a simple headstone in Coventry,

Hale is honored today for his willingness to sacrifice his life in service to his country. This statue of Nathan Hale stands at City Hall in New York City.

Connecticut. He wanted it to stand as a memorial to his son. The inscription to Nathan Hale read, "resign'd his life a sacrifice to his country's liberty."[38] Richard Hale's tribute to his son still stands today as a reminder of the courage of America's fallen heroes.

Nathan Hale's example and sacrifice embodies the patriotic spirit of America. Although his story is adventurous and exciting, there was nothing romantic about Hale's life. He was a simple, intelligent, courageous man, doing what he felt was right. Even when faced with death, Hale only regretted the thought that he could not do more. Today, his life is a symbol of selfless dedication to the cause of liberty.

In 1846, the first monument to Hale was dedicated in Coventry. This monument was one of the first pillars in America built to honor a national hero. Several other statues have also been built in his honor. Fittingly, in 1985, the Connecticut legislature chose Nathan Hale as the official state hero. He is remembered as one of the many great martyrs of the American Revolution.

Test Your Knowledge

I Who was the first member of the Hale family to learn of Nathan's death?

   a. His father.

   b. His stepmother.

   c. His brother Enoch.

   d. His stepsister Alice.

2 In December 1776, Washington's troops enjoyed an important victory over Hessian troops in what town?

   a. Williamsburg, Virginia.

   b. Valley Forge, Pennsylvania.

   c. Saratoga, New York.

   d. Trenton, New Jersey.

3 What battle convinced the French to support the Patriots in the war?

   a. The Battle at Brandywine Creek.

   b. The Battle at Saratoga.

   c. The Battle at Yorktown.

   d. The Battle of Guilford Courthouse.

4 At Yorktown, Washington combined his army with forces from what other country?

   a. France.

   b. Holland.

   c. Spain.

   d. Germany.

5 What treaty brought an end to the Revolutionary War?

   a. The Treaty of London.

   b. The Treaty of Versailles.

   c. The Treaty of Paris.

   d. The Treaty of Philadelphia.

ANSWERS: 1. c; 2. d; 3. b; 4. a; 5. c

1755 Hale is born in Coventry, Connecticut on June 6.

1767 Great Britain passes the Townshend Acts, placing taxes on glass, paper, paint, lead, and tea.

1769 Hale enters Yale College in New Haven.

1770 Five colonists are killed by British soldiers in the Boston Massacre on March 5.

1773 Hale graduates from Yale College and accepts a teaching position in East Haddam, Connecticut; Boston Tea Party is held on December 16.

1774 Hale takes a new teaching job at Union Grammar School in New London; British close Boston Harbor;

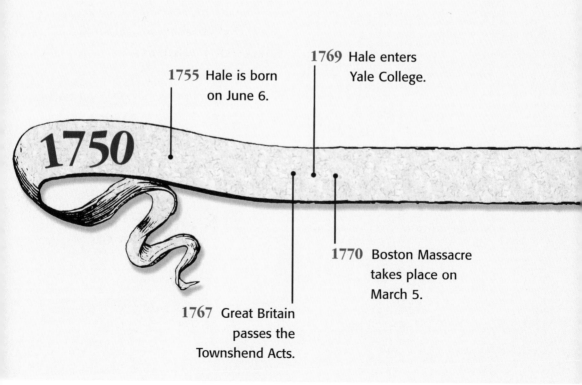

1755 Hale is born on June 6.

1769 Hale enters Yale College.

1750

1767 Great Britain passes the Townshend Acts.

1770 Boston Massacre takes place on March 5.

the First Continental Congress meets in Philadelphia in December.

1775 Battles of Lexington and Concord are fought in April, beginning the Revolutionary War; Hale joins the Connecticut Army; he is promoted to captain in September.

1776 Hale steals a British sloop in the East River; joins Colonel Thomas Knowlton's Rangers; volunteers to become a spy behind British lines in New York; Hale is betrayed by his cousin and captured by the British on September 21; he is hanged the following day as an American spy.

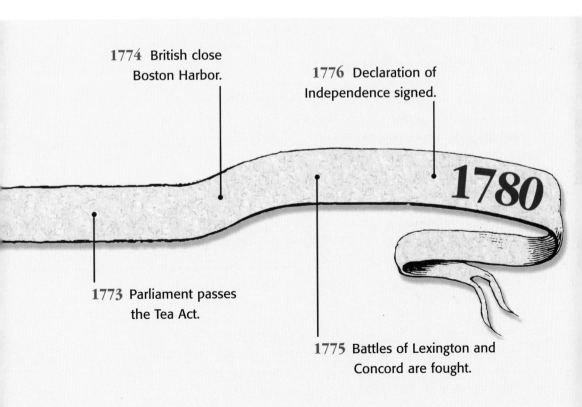

1774 British close Boston Harbor.

1776 Declaration of Independence signed.

1780

1773 Parliament passes the Tea Act.

1775 Battles of Lexington and Concord are fought.

Notes

CHAPTER 1
Surrender or Die!

1 George Dudley Seymour, *Documentary Life of Nathan Hale* (New Haven, Conn.: privately published, 1941), 317.

2 Ibid.

3 Ibid.

CHAPTER 2
A Special Lad

4 Charlotte Molyneux Holloway, *Nathan Hale: The Martyr-hero of the Revolution* (New York: Perkins Book Company, 1902), 9.

5 Ibid.

6 Ibid., 9–10.

7 Ibid., 12–13.

8 Ibid., 24.

9 Connecticut Society of the Sons of the American Revolution, Nathan Hale Schoolhouse. http://www.ctssar.org/sites/e_haddam_hale_schoolhouse.htm.

10 Ibid.

CHAPTER 4
The Shot Heard 'Round the World

11 David Hackett Fischer, *Paul Revere's Ride* (New York: Oxford University Press, 1994), 109.

12 Holloway, 98–100.

CHAPTER 5
For Independence

13 Henry Phelps Johnston, *Nathan Hale, 1776* (New Haven, Conn.: Yale University Press, 1914), 65.

14 Holloway, 109–110.

15 Connecticut Society of the Sons of the American Revolution, Nathan Hale Schoolhouse. http://www.ctssar.org/sites/e_haddam_hale_schoolhouse.htm.

16 Seymour, 181.

17 Ibid., 317.

18 Holloway, 137.

19 Ibid.

CHAPTER 6
A Spy!

20 Ibid., 146.

21 Ibid., 148.

22 Seymour, 317.

23 Holloway, 162.

24 Ibid., 163–164.

25 Ibid., 165.

CHAPTER 7
But One Life

26 Ibid., 171.

27 Ibid., 173.

28 Ibid.

29 Ibid., 173–174.

30 Ibid., 174.

31 Ibid.

32 Ibid., 185–186.

33 Ibid., 190.

34 Ibid., 194.

35 Seymour, 454.

36 Holloway, 196.

CHAPTER 8
A New Nation

37 Seymour, 295.

38 Ibid., 302.

Bibliography

Darrow, Jane. *Nathan Hale: A Story of Loyalties*. New York: Century Company, 1932.

Holloway, Charlotte Molyneux. *Nathan Hale: The Martyr-hero of the Revolution*. New York: The Perkins Book Company, 1902.

Johnston, Henry Phelps. *Nathan Hale, 1776*. New Haven, Conn.: Yale University Press, 1914.

Root, Jean Christie. *Nathan Hale*. New York: The Macmillan Company, 1925.

Seymour, George Dudley. *Documentary Life of Nathan Hale*. New Haven, Conn.: privately published, 1941.

Zinn, Howard. *A People's History of the United States: 1492–Present*. New York: HarperPerennial, 1995.

WEBSITES
Nathan Hale Schoolhouse

www.ctssar.org/sites/e_haddam_hale_schoolhouse.htm

Further Reading

Lough, Loree. *Nathan Hale*. Philadelphia: Chelsea House, 2000.

Todd, Anne. *The Revolutionary War*. Mankato, Minn.: Capstone Press, 2001.

WEBSITES

Kid Info: The American Revolution
www.kidinfo.com/American_History/American_Revolution.html

Liberty! The American Revolution
www.pbs.org/ktca/liberty

Spy Letters of the American Revolution
www.si.umich.edu/spies/index-gallery.html

Index

Picture Credits

page:

3: © Bettmann/CORBIS

4: © Library of Congress,
LC-USC4-572

14: © Library of Congress

18: © Art Resource, NY

25: © Library of Congress,
LC-USZC4-1582

31: © Todd Gipstein/CORBIS

35: © Library of Congress,
LC-USZC4-7216

47: © Bettmann/CORBIS

50: © Bettmann/CORBIS

60: © Bettmann/CORBIS

66: © Bettmann/CORBIS

76: © Library of Congress,
LC-USZC4-2135

85: © CORBIS

91: © Library of Congress,
LC-USZ62-45179

100: © Bettmann/CORBIS

105: © Profiles in History/CORBIS

108: © Lee Snider/Photo Images/
CORBIS

110: © Farrell Grehan/CORBIS

Cover: © Lee Snider/Photo Images/CORBIS

RACHEL A. KOESTLER-GRACK has worked with nonfiction books as an editor and writer since 1999. She lives on a farm near Glencoe, Minnesota. During her career, she has worked extensively in several different historical periods, including the colonial era, the Civil War era, the Great Depression, and the civil rights movement.